Blend In

by Alexander Sanchez
illustrated by Anthony Lewis

Practice Decodable 30

McGraw Hill Education

Bothell, WA • Chicago, IL • Columbus, OH • New York, NY

MHEonline.com

Send all inquiries to:
McGraw-Hill Education
8787 Orion Place
Columbus, OH 43240

ISBN: 978-0-02-136281-3
MHID: 0-02-136281-5

Printed in China.

8 9 10 11 12 DSS 27 26 25 24 23

See a red fox at rest.

Is it just a stem? It is a tan insect!

A big cat blends in. See its spots!

Next, see a frog. Is it there?

Look down there! Is it a log?

Ten kids can blend in!